ALSO BY WALTER BENTON

NEVER A GREATER NEED

THIS IS A BORZOI BOOK

PUBLISHED IN NEW YORK

BY ALFRED A. KNOPF

THIS IS
MY BELOVED

ALFRED A. KNOPF *NEW YORK*

1954

THIS IS
MY BELOVED

BY WALTER BENTON

PUBLISHED FEBRUARY 1, 1943

Pocket Edition,
Reset and printed from new plates, August 1949
Reprinted three times
Fifth printing, June 1954

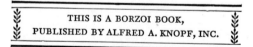

THIS IS A BORZOI BOOK,
PUBLISHED BY ALFRED A. KNOPF, INC.

for Lillian

I

Because hate is legislated, written into

the primer and the testament,

shot into our blood and brain like

> vaccine or vitamins

Because our day is of time, of hours—and the

> clock-hand turns,

closes the circle upon us: and black

> timeless night

sucks us in like quicksand, receives us totally—

without a raincheck or a parachute,

> a key to heaven or the last long look

I need love more than ever now . . . I need

> your love—

I need love more

than hope or money . . . wisdom or a drink

Because slow negative death withers the world—
  and only yes can turn the tide
Because love has your face and body, and your
  hands are tender
and your mouth is sweet—
and God has made no other eyes like yours.

You rise out of sleep like a growing thing
rises out of the garden soil.
Two leaves part to be your mouth,

> two tender seedleaves—

and your eyes are wonderfully starlike,
your eyes are luminous and soft as the velvet of

> pansies.

Darling, good morning.

Our arms are empty of each other

> for a moment only.

How beautifully you turn . . . your mouth tilts

> to let my kisses in.

Lie still . . . we shall be longer.

We need so little room, we two—

thus on a single pillow . . . as we move nearer,

nearer heaven—

until I burst inside you like a screaming rocket.

Then we are quietly apart returning to this earth.

Some see you in similes: Helen's rich curves,
colors autumn has.
You please them as an opium dream pleases,
       or you smile like the sun is rising—
or you walk proudly like a woman courted.

But I see you best unrelated . . . with not a
       metaphor to your name:
your hair not like the silk of corn or spiders
       but like your hair,
your mouth resembling
       nothing so wonderfully much
       as your own mouth.

Why should I say you are like a slender
  waterbird on wing?
This is but a slide of you, a fraction.
Or that your thighs are lilies—lilies are cold,
lilies are neither quick nor scented, they do not
  stain the night with
velvet musk—
they cannot fire love . . . and quench it.

I mean . . . compliments become you
as tinsel becomes a tall, snow covered cedar
  in a mountain cedar wood.

Your words are born, not spoken.
Dimensional, soft-vowelled words, palpable to
      the eye or to the fingertip:
exquisitely curved as the young that flowers
      conceive.

Often have I watched your lips shape words—
      and your tongue nudge them out
like small birds not wholly certain of their
      wings.
Your sweetest words are those shaped ovally like
      plums or wild birds' eggs.

And the long bright ribbons you laugh—
the multitudes of hyacinth and bluebells.

When I see words like soft grey catkins

I know they are of love . . . whatever else

my ears register.

And because your mouth is like the flesh of

ripe fig,

often I take your words unsaid—

as the brown honey-bear slips his red tongue

into the nest of sleeping bees to take out honey.

And the sweet natural taste,

the pussy-willow feel of your words is lovelier

than their shape or music.

ENTRY *May 25*

    All right, sulk.

But as you sit, so . . . knees high—

the wild spiral feathers

accentuating the meeting of your thighs,

like dark grass grown in too rich a soil—

you are beautifully eloquent.

Or when your gown loosens, falls off the small

fierce faces of your breasts, as the cowl falls

off the face of the hunter's falcon . . . I attend,

        nerve-naked.

I memorize you . . . walking as if to music.

Your dress

11

lies against the cheeks and hollow of your thighs
        like running water.
Your breasts nod yes each step. Your slow
involute hips cradle the eternal synonym for God.

The dress censors not a syllable of you.
Articulate eyes wink from your breasts and belly,
signal from your throat—
beckon from your knees, your waist, your mobile
        shoulders.

Yes, your body makes eyes at me from every
        salient,
promises warm lavish promises—
curved, colored, finished in warm velvet,
        like baby rabbits.

Your eyes never opened after the last kiss.
We had loved hard—
it's all over your throat and hair,
it lies on your mouth like a wild red flower:
it's on your cheeks and forehead in technicolor.

The wonderful strength of your thighs is back to
        gentle beauty.
Your nipples contract, gather in like blossoms
for the night. Your hand, half-sleeping, finds me—
your touch is very dear.

Now you are all sleep, alone with yourself—
        and a tall blue fence around you:
not a tendon taut, not a secret secret,

you are all sleep and alone in a warm and velvet
world—

many an idle dream is looking for a home of
sleep like yours to happen in.

ENTRY *June 11*

Why am I looking at you like this?
Only because I want to remember this, all this—
the musty glasses and the checkered tablecloth,

cigarette butts, burnt matches, spilled beer and
crumpled napkins.
The juke box—
and the sailor with his hand inside the girl's
dress.
The strong urine smell—
and the whores and fairies watching like spiders.

And the way the fingered piano eggs the dancers
on to exaggerate their coupling
gestures.

The recorded orgasm of the saxophone—

Hey, bartender!
Isn't it about time we had one on the house?

Darling—
oh, I want to remember you always,
                everywhere—
in a tavern or in church, asleep or taking bath,
I must not ever forget the look in your eyes
                when you had drunk
and wanted to hurry home and be loved to sleep.

Sleep late, nobody cares what time it is.

Sunday morning, coffee in bed . . . then love
>   with coffee flavored kisses.

And your tongue dripping honey like a ripe fig.

I have been hours awake looking at

you lithely at rest in the free natural way
>   rivers bed and clouds shape.

Your bedgown gathers up your full round thighs,
>   rolls over your hips.

Your breasts are snub like children's faces

and your navel deep as a god's eye.

Yes, your lips match your teats beautifully, rose
>   and rose. The hair

of your arm's hollow and where your thighs
      meet
agree completely, being brown and soft to look at
      like a nest of field mice.
Praise be the walls that shelter you from eyes
      that are not mine!

Love, not prayers, shall be our offering this day.
We shall praise God with absolute embraces,
      our bodies shall sing Him
in His own incomparable tongue.
Prayer is humbleness, I cannot be humble with
      the wealth of you beside me.

ENTRY *June 17*

Somewhere cities crouch . . . cower—

(Move nearer me). The violet sky
parasols us . . . and from the incandescent
      noon
the sun pours into the moist, open earth.
The woods are sweet and bedwarm as your
      breasts in the morning.
Somewhere a clock is timing us . . . hurry—
with the grass still under us and the sun
kissing us pink with lover's lips, not scavenger's
      teeth—

come, love me.

You smile yes and your lips part, fill out like
       leeches.
Yes is a darting hummingbird inside your throat
and in your armpits yes is sweeter than
the ground mint staining your warm naked
       thighs.
Your breasts are wonderfully alive under my
       kisses.

Tremble against me, if we must spill blood,
let it flow thickly like yellow honey on a tongue,
let it meet as in a flower
       and the petals close upon it—
yes, let it live,
timecapsuled in a new generation of you and me.

Were I Pygmalion or God . . . I would
make you exactly as you are, in all dimensions.
From your warm hair to your intimate toes
would you be wholly in your own image.

I would change nothing, add or take away.
The same full red flower
> would model for your mouth—
and from the same seashore would I bring
the small translucent earshapes of your ears.

O the lovely throat that I could duplicate!
The tender arms!
I would shape your breasts the shape
> of the hungry little faces they are **now**

21

and tip them with the same quick mouths.

I could not make your eyes deeper than they are,
nor softer to look into—
nor could I turn your hips, your thighs, your
        belly in a sweeter curve:
nor indent the hollows of your loins
more tenderly—or store more honey there or
        fire.

How would I name you . . . need you ask?
You know.

        By the scarlet and the blue you wear
when love is upon you,
by the yellow tongues—
by the warm white fragrance, by the slender
        leaves.

Last night

we entered our bed through opposite **doors.**

Hours

we lay awake, entrenched, before the trapdoor

gave

and we were hurtling down in jerky sleep.

When we suddenly awoke,

our bodies were together in the warm bed lap—

and I was taking deep swollen kisses out of your

brimming mouth.

Your lips cushioned the inherent murder in your

teeth.

My body grew to fit your body . . . and the

opened

blossoms of you were flaming, full . . . and
    making honey.

There in the jungle twilight, stark naked god
slipped in between us, and the lightning struck—
and in the light I saw you
you were lovelier by many years than yesterday.

Today, your mind moved back into your face
    willing away your last night's beauty.
And the hard mask of resolution
lies dull upon you . . . like a bad make-up.

II

I stood long where you left me.

Night was all around me and the stars pecked at it
with fierce acetylene silver beaks.

A little thin moon scarred the sky.

Then I walked, my arm around the emptiness
of you beside me.

And because you were total in my eyes, like
sudden blindness,

I saw only you. You were my purpose and my
way,

you were the bright articulate lights
and the dark lonely streets,

you were each door and window, and every
passing face.

27

And because you were indelible in my blood and
　　　brain
in infinite copies—
without drink or delirium my mind conceived you,
my senses registered you dimensionally.

And it was beautiful, O then it was beautiful
in a high beautiful city,
in a tall lighted beautiful world—
the moon was young and the stars winked like
　　　fireflies in tall grass.
Night was a jewelled tent around us, and we
　　　were wonderfully alone
and sleepy . . . as we always are just after love.

ENTRY *July 26*

The thin skeletal moon reminded me
and the sharp electric stars, when I walked to
      meet you.
And meeting you,
your face—grim and implacable—reminded me.

And the studied way you controlled pleasure,
even when we had drunk, danced, heard swing
      music:
even when you read my new poem to you.
All these reminded me. A month had passed—
a month . . . by the gaunt red moon,
like the mark of an incandescent thumbnail.

Your mind's cosmetic lay frightfully upon you:
muddied your eyes and settled on your mouth.
Entered your skin like acid.
How will you be when you have fully torn the
rainbows off my eyes?

Ah, we will be poor then, you and I—sorry and
wrong, alone and poor—
for all our righteousness and love we may have
found in others.
Yes, I will be poor—what else not having you
can mean to me?

And as for you, all the things you cannot ever be,
you are

only because my love is like the magic touch
of stars.
You wear my love, and all who see you say:
how beautifully his love becomes her!

1

Each season of each year
I will be forgetting you all over. Each season.
Every year.
I will need to forget you each summer, spring—
autumn and winter.

Each summer I will be forgetting:
you forever naked, you brown with the sun's fire,
you moving in massive adagio like a seal turning
in water.
You lying in the sun . . . or looking darling
in a cotton dress.
You—and the kites. Connecticut . . . and you.

Autumn, I will be forgetting meeting you,
and the first long kiss on the green bedlam hill,
under the rash of stars—
I could not leave your mouth . . . remember?
And the garret rooms we lived in. The bitter-
      sweet
we gathered, and the rich red sumac, in the high
hectic woods where the air was ripe apples
      and the colors chrysanthemum.

Each winter there will be long evenings together
      to forget, reading or talking—
having friends. Greenup on the Ohio.
The sweetness of you in bed—and growing
      sleepy in each other's arms.

And you returning to me each morning "for one
        minute only"
nakedly, for warmth—
your mouth full of cool mint toothpaste kisses.

Spring will be the hardest to forget, with lovers
        everywhere—
O spring will be hard . . . forgetting the early
violets along the Hocking,
hitching to Marietta—
and the lamb that broke the fold to follow us.
Love we made beside the river, lying on
        the grass . . .
how beautiful you were,
pale-green where you showed naked to the moon,

your eyes were tearbright, your eyes were full of
        moonlight and of stars
and you were wonderfully warm and trembling
        when you let me in.

2

I will be forgetting you each day and every hour.
Each night and day, each hour something
wonderful and dear of you will ring my heart
        and knock upon my mind.

Each time I hear Gilbert and Sullivan—Strauss,
        see ginkgo trees, read
Lewis Carroll: see flowering dogwood or smell
locust, acacia, sweet honeysuckle, lily of the
        valley . . . or wild roses.

I shall forever be forgetting the quick, happy
       kisses,
like samples, when my own lips could never fully
       capture yours.
And the deep, ravenous kisses, when I awoke
       wanting you at night.

Sunday will be the hardest to forget,
late Sunday mornings, with your sleep rich body
and your hardly opened eyes terribly tender.
The articulate wordlessness of your lips and
       tongue . . . and the natural way
you raised your gown and fitted yourself to me.

O I drew love like honey-steeped wine

from every mouth of you—and when we had

loved our fill,

we laughed, and we were very hungry.

Then we ate fruit with cream and sugar, bacon—

sausages and cakes with rich brown maple syrup

and drank strong, fragrant coffee.

3

Each time I know beauty it shall be through you.

When joy lifts me high—or sorrow breaks me,

when I love again . . . my

senses conditioned to you will be forgetting you

anew.

Each kiss that fills my mouth shall fill it with

your lips—

yes, each time my eyelids crumble and close
>under blood's fired impact,
when love strikes home, yours will be the mouth

and yours the disengaging arms:
your heart it will be leaping in your throat and
>beating in your thighs.
Your relieved breasts.
Your simmering loins. Your soft, happy eyes.

I will be forgetting you in silence and in song—
>in silence will I dream
dreams of you too wonderful to dare aloud,
and of words I shall not use for anyone but you
>I shall make poems.

When a star falls, I shall wish for you.

When the moon is new, I shall wish for you.

When a bird looks into my window, when a leaf
        falls before me,

when I find a fern in flower, I shall wish for you.

And when the autumn lays out her lavish colors,

her warm brown, ripe yellow,

her exciting red all over the hills and fields,
        like a lovely

woman undressing . . . I shall look for you.

ENTRY *August 22*

As the world gathers momentum
toward nihilation on all fronts, we walk apart,
each to his own
lonely end—not hand in hand as lovers walk.

Yet I would enter time's infinite pages
more happily with you than in the company of
Christs and Dantes—comets and constellations!

Darling . . . before the distance widens beyond
reach and sight, look this way—
give me your hand, that the stars may say of us:

The last we saw of them was when they kissed,

then beautifully naked walked as if into a sea

of bright blue water—

leaving their bodies like old clothes upon the

shore.

The white full moon like a great
beautiful whore solicits over the city, eggs the
      lovers on, the haves,
walking in twos to their beds and to their mating.

I walk alone. Slowly. No hurry. Nobody's
      waiting.
My love who loved me (she said) is gone.
                My love is gone.

And I walk alone. It's goodnight time—the haves
are everywhere, in parked cars and passing
      taxis—
the still abstracted figures pressed against walls
and niched in dark doorways . . . each two

arm-hooped into one body rigid with joy.

A lighted window holds me like high voltage.

I see . . . cupped in the bed's white palm, the
        haves—

O she is beautiful, her breasts are white dogwood
        and her thighs barked poplar growing

out of the dark-matted jungle of her crotch.

He is kissing her, interminably her mouth—and

one by one each breast is carried to the lips
        with tender violence.

Now he lays his hand to her secret body.

Her frantic thighs invite invasion.

He covers her, enters . . . turns god
        —and my eyelids fall.

It was like something done in fever
when nothing fits, mind into mind nor body into
        body—
when nothing meets or equals,
when dimensions lie and perceptions go haywire.

With what an alien sense my fingers curved
about her breasts and searched the tangled dark
where love lay hiding!
I closed my eyes better to imagine you—
but the rehearsed body would not ratify the
        mind's deception.

The kisses of her mouth, the rhythm natural to
        love, and

the exciting musk with which love haloes itself—
these thwarted my imagination. Her love, too,
      was centered and intent,

it did not reach her eyes and forehead, or light
      her throat as your love did—
it did not fill the room or spread all over
      the ceiling of the sky.
It did not span the years and miles
      and hold hands with beast and God.

Nor did her thighs rise with that splendid grade
      I stroked from memory.
Her body met me unlike your body, and I entered
the heaven of her uneasily—and could not stay,
for my heart, being yours, released no blood to
      make ready for love.

I saw autumn today, incipiently, on the
sunset and the leaf—
in the spontaneous whitecaps shingling the bay
and the window-displayed chrysanthemums and
      asters.

I saw its night's watercolor leavings on the
      cottonwood and the maple
and heard its voice in the locust's highpowered
      chatter in the camouflaged somewhere.

Ah! fierce exhilaration flows through me like
      dry current.
Soon we shall walk on the sunny side of the
      street,

hold hands, mingle in bed for warmth.
Autumn is our season . . . yours and mine.

See, I have lain long naked in the sun to match
       your body.
We shall look beautiful lying side by side.
The stain of the season is rich upon you,
only your breasts are white as the winter
       grouse—
you have not shown them to the sun,
       nor the low of your belly
where you are white, soft and darkfeathered.

When all the poems on the theme have been
written
and all the night and day dreams dreamt without
        prophecy or fulfilment.
When hope sustains us no longer, nor being
        drunk
or busy or therapeutically in love keeps us from
        remembering.

When our new interests, our richer lives, require
quotes to qualify their meanings:
and however hard we try, we can exploit our
grievances no further to fortify our resolutions—

what will we do to keep madness sulking in the
    brain?

When we have forgotten even why we parted, if
    we ever knew it at all—
remembering, however, when we could sleep
    naked
and be warm together, kiss—though with a cold:
when even baby-talk became you . . . yes,
and everything I said was sweet or funny
and everything you did was beautiful.

See, I alter nothing. This is you and I in
dark-gray lead, on plain white paper.
No flattering magenta colors. No accompaniment
in minor key—or brilliant arpeggios.

Just sit as you are, or stand—and do whatever
you are doing,
while the kodak shutter winks you into
permanence.
Just turn the last flight of stairway as I open
the door . . . and say hello.

Just slip into your nightdress, stumble into bed,
say goodnight and go soft all over.

Turn, drape yourself over me like a lissome
        python,
our smooth bodies touching everywhere.
Sleep rising from you lulls me like the sweet
        smoke of hashish.

Leave everything exactly as it is:
The undone hair clouding the pillow and the
        small
ears lost snugly somewhere in the clouds.
The little blue veins under your breasts and
the brown birthmarks inside your thighs.
The bittersweet climbing the beech
and the partridge berry trailing on the ground.
The early crocus and the second-flowering
        hawthorn.

You see, this needs no retouching. The colors
are natural and the shape universal. Therefore
I shall never forget you, nor will your memory
be ever free of me.
For your arms are my home and my arms the
     circle
you cannot leave . . . however far you go.

ENTRY *September 27*

How dark is the river! How still and dark
with deep, slow-moving darkness!
The seagulls, dreaming violence, cried me awake
with their strangely anguished voices—
like the voices of women being taken in love.

Here where nights are deep as clear deep water
and the sky spawns stars abundantly,

   teeming with golden inflorescence:
away from the world we lived in . . . the streets
we walked together and the roofs we flew

   kites from.
The doors we entered and the bed we loved on.

Far from the late sunny autumns, the walks
            under the McGuffy Elms
and the coffeeshop where we played truant,
convocation hours—I watch the season go with
            you,
the summer close,
and the year's end draw nearer,
            and the world's—

Hear the crows heckle the strawman in the
            cornpatch across the river?
It is so strange, this my need of you. Yesterday
I gathered seashells at Compo Beach, but I had
            no one to show them to.

And when I saw blue heron fishing in the
    Saugatuck shallows—
I cried to Cora: "Lillian, look!"

ENTRY *October 15*

Everyone is sleeping. Nothing wakes.
The woods are motionless. The wind is down to
    a whisper.
Sleep hums like current—yes, audibly—
    through the bright steel night.

The evening star rises like a flaming wick.
Hills fit into hills like lovers, their great dark
    straddling thighs
clasping still greater darkness where they meet.

A star breaks, arcs down the night—like God
striking a match across the cathedral ceiling.

Therefore I wish—see my lips move, making

      your name.

It is so still,

so still . . . I am sure that you must hear me.

ENTRY *October 17*

This is how the sun rose over Paine
  Mountain:
the high horizon paled, inching upwards
like a stripteaser lifting her dress to show her
  white body.
Cloud-fragments pinkened like nipples, and the
  icy ledges refracted the white—
raying out like the Resurrection.

The height of the mountain later, appeared the
  sun.

And this is how it set:
all day it slunk along about a witch's height,

when suddenly (it must have stumbled)

it dropped out of sight somewhere

in Northfield Hills, where the Mad River is.

And the lit clouds fanned out in tall,

fantastic branches of plum and apple heavy with

blossom—

and the sky was seagreen behind them.

Then I remembered—you loved apple blossoms,

and I reached out over the dun, amber hills and

broke off large sprays, abundant with sweet air

and soft colors.

I shall give them to you some spring, when our

love comes home.

Entry *October 24*

The Green Hills sprawl in the last sun
of autumn. This morning I lay on a hillside
and the sun was warm—
it was like lying naked under your naked kisses—

and eleven years of you moved through my
      memory,
eleven years walked, laughed, lay, loved me—
ate, drank, quarrelled . . . made up.
The sweat of the leaves under my feet
      excited me.
Leaves left where they fall are sweeter in the air
than crushed green mint or fallen apples.

O what is this that drives me so, as if to keep
some destined date!

The sun lowers. I smoke hard to check the jitters.
The train drives a shrieking wedge between the
hills.
I close my eyes.
I move to give you the window seat beside me—
though two states lie between us, and four long
terrible months.

III

My heart swells, bulges . . . my heart
presses against my lungs, I cannot breathe—
it rises to my throat and throttles my words.
O it will burst sky-high, surely, and a cloud of
        starlings will fly out!
A swarm of luminous moths and boisterous
        starlings.

Why do they stare at me as I stride the Village
        streets,
crossing the crossings against the lights and
        recognizing no one?

Are my eyes too bright? Is my head too high?
Or does it really show, that kiss—

does it sit on my lips like a moth on a leaf,

has your kiss blossomed on my mouth into a

scarlet flower?

How long—how long can I live this night!

Look . . . the clouds shine,

darling, how did you do it? The wind is soft,

the rain is beautiful—

what did you do to the wind . . . and the rain

and the clouds?

And to me? See, I am drunk . . . high—

I am drunk on you as on a reefer!

We will cross here where the street is crowded

that I may hold your hand.

We will ride the subways that we may sit

touching—

that there be no distance between us.

Speak, that I may fill my ears with you.

Stay near me, so—that I may fill my lungs with
you.

Come home with me . . . that I may fill my
arms with you.

Come where only I can see you—and undo your
dress about your throat,

and my lips will make the nipples of your breasts
burst open like acorns

planted in warm spring soil. Come home with me—

lift your dress high . . . your thighs will light
my room with moonlight

and the hair in the pocket of them

will recall to me the darkness of firs and
      larches in the dark mountain passes.

If only I could fit my life's time into these
      hours—
that I might say:
"I was with her from eight to twelve o'clock—
      and years passed"!

    I waited years today . . . one year for
every hour,
all day—though I knew you could not come
       till night, I waited—
and nothing else in this God's hell meant
       anything.

I had everything you love . . . shellfish and
       saltsticks, watercress, black olives.
Wine (for the watch I pawned), real cream
       for our coffee.
Smoked cheese, currants in port, preserved wild
       cherries.

I bought purple asters from a pushcart florist
    and placed them where
they would be between us—
imagining your lovely face among them.

But you did not come . . . you did not come.
You did not come.
And I left the table lit and your glass filled—
    and my glass empty,
and went out into the night looking for you.

The glittering pile, Manhattan, swarmed like
    an uncovered dung heap.
Along the waterfront
manlike shapes, all shoulders and collar, walked
    stiffly like shadow figures.

Later, the half-moon rose.

Everywhere the windows falling dark.

By St. Mark's church, under the iron fence,

      a girl was crying.

And the old steeple was mouldy with moonlight,

and I was tired . . . and very lonely.

IV

I knew your eyes by heart after the very
first reading.
I could repeat them in detail, remembering their
elements in pearls and moonstones—
in the dark wing of a starling and the bright
morning faces of asters.

I learned your hair many ways—by the musk
and visually,
by the Braille touch . . . I could tell which part
of your body grew it:
the underhair fringing your face was sensitive
like thin smoke in a draft—
between your thighs it was natural and crisp
like the hearts of lettuce.

After one fitting only I could cup my hands just so—as if they held your face.

Blindfolded, I could kiss a thousand mouths and know your lips.

I could tell time by your mouth's kisses, feel rich red colors,

taste sun-ripe fruits . . . and know the seasons of the year.

I took your body like a glass of sweet milk at bedtime.

And my eyelids let go at the hinges when
      I entered you

You were all I and all of me was you—my senses rhymed with your senses, and our bodies made music and gave light . . . as all things absolute.

What is it that happened?

Now that you are gone (and why) I feel I never

knew you—

though you fill me with terrible wonder, like

the onset of madness.

What enslaving cocktail have I sucked
from your full mouth

> to leave me so totally yours!

The red pulp of your kisses is sweet on my

> tongue

as the red ripe melon meat—
yes, even **now** . . . though remembered only,
though you are marketing your love.

I have looked too long upon you, too long . . .
and with so much love, strangers can see you

> in my face—

as the sun and vivid colors leave an after-image

> in the eyes.

There are no stars tonight to get my
bearing by.
What time is it? What season? What year?
The sky sags . . . bellies. The city gargles
      dust in the streets.

I am lost on an island somewhere between two
      rivers.
Blind buildings are all around me and the earth
is covered with flat stones. And over me, the low
      dark roof—
the harbor's lifted morass—and the belchings
      of many chimneys.

NOTE

This book was set on the Linotype in Bodoni
Book, *a printing-type so called after Giambat-
tista Bodoni, a celebrated printer and type de-
signer of Rome and Parma (1740–1813). Bodoni's innovations in printing-type style were
a greater degree of contrast in the "thick and
thin" elements of the letters, and a sharper and
more angular finish of details.*

*The book was composed, printed, and bound
by H. Wolff, New York. Typography and bind-
ing based on designs by* W. A. DWIGGINS.